Follow Your Dreams

07 08 09 10 11 SDB 10 9 8 7 6 5 4 3 2

ISBN-13: 978-0-7407-6364-9
ISBN-10: 0-7407-6364-4

Library of Congress Control Number: 2006931989

www.andrewsmcmeel.com

Licensed by Creatif
www.coedikit.com

ATTENTION: SCHOOLS AND BUSINESSES
Andrews McMeel books are available at quantity discounts with
bulk purchase for educational, business, or sales promotional use. For
information, please write to: Special Sales Department, Andrews McMeel
Publishing, LLC, 4520 Main Street, Kansas City, Missouri 64111.

Follow Your Dreams

(Except for That One Where You Go to Work Naked and Dance the Polka)

Cheryl Caldwell
a Co-edikit book

**Andrews McMeel
Publishing, LLC**

Kansas City

Sometimes things aren't at all like
they feel . . .

It is as
bad as you think,

and they
are
out to get you.

and you have to be careful not to take everything at face value.

A day without
sunshine . . .
is like night,
actually.

and you just need to exercise a little common sense.

If
you feel blue,

start
breathing
again.

There will be days when it's hard to put your best foot forward . . .

Wait a minute . . .
I need
to put on my
"Gosh-I-Really-Care"
face.

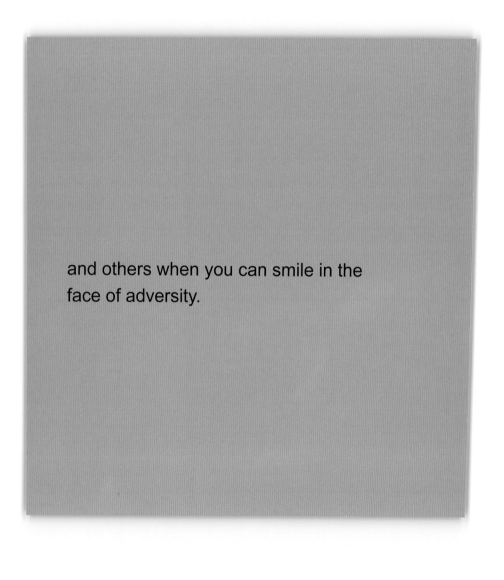

and others when you can smile in the face of adversity.

So look on the bright side.

It's better
to have
loved and lost,
than to have spent
the rest of my
life with that
psycho!

Adopt a new attitude.

Don't hate me
because
I'm beautiful.

Discover your true self, whoever that may be.

Believe in your own self-worth.

You can't
afford me.

Don't be afraid to admit your faults.

Discover who you are deep down.

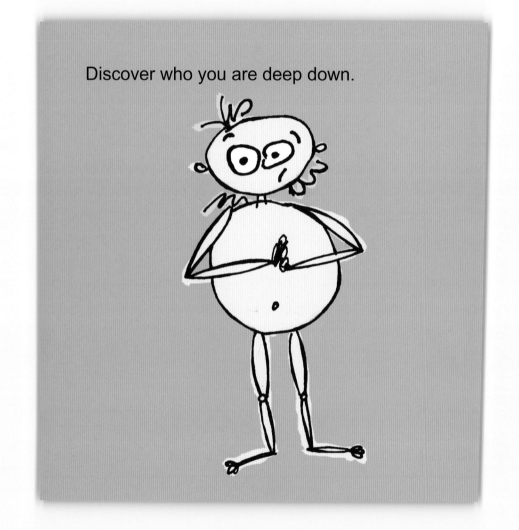

Underneath
it all . . .

I'm pretty much
naked.

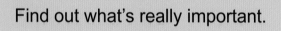

Find out what's really important.

Shoes are life.

The rest is just accessories.

Explore the many facets of your being.

Celebrate your talents . . .

Support
Your
Local Hooker

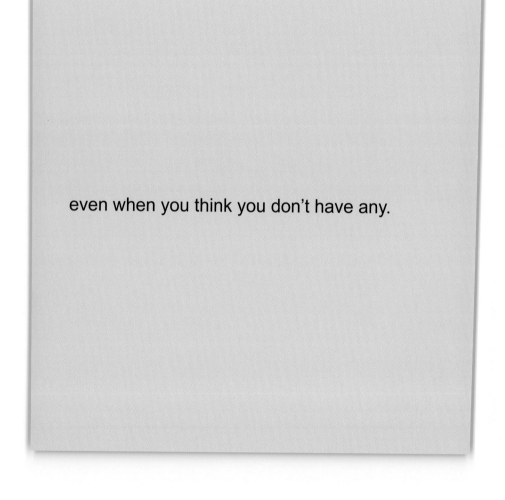

even when you think you don't have any.

Regular Garden
Variety Ho

Don't let negative people bring you down.

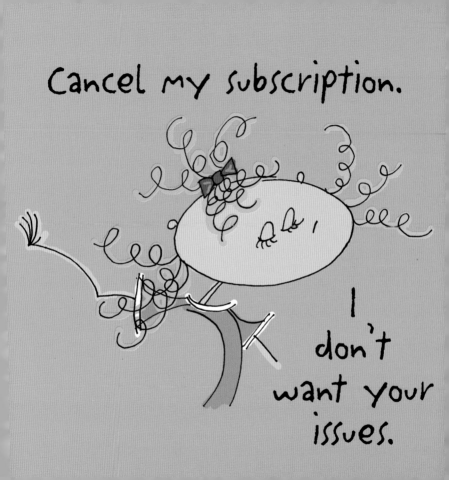

Remember, just because everyone seems to have something to say . . .

doesn't mean they know what they're talking about.

Stick for Brains

Don't be afraid to march to the beat of your own drummer . . .

I live in
my
own little world,
but it's OK. . . .

They know
me here!

even if you're the only one who hears it.

You're
just jealous

because

the voices
only talk to me.

That doesn't mean you can't be
accommodating . . .

or polite.

It's
been lovely,

but
I have to
scream now.

You just need to know when to put your
foot down . . .

and when to let things go.

Keep your mind open for small surprises . . .

and things you knew all along.

You don't have to be an expert in everything . . .

I may not know karate, but I know crazy!

but be ready to learn something new
every day.

But whatever you do, don't take yourself too seriously . . .

What if
the
hokey-pokey
really
is
what it's all about?

even when other people do.

You're out of
your gourd!

Life is too important to rush through.

I consider

ON TIME

to be

when I get there.

Find joy in all the many pleasures life has to offer.

Hail to
the
Mocha
Latte

Kick up your heels.

So many
parties . . .
so little time.

Celebrate your victories.

ROCK is dead.

Long live PAPER
and SCISSORS!

And don't be afraid to take a stand.

I'm not a vegetarian
because I love animals.

I'm a vegetarian
because I hate plants.

Things may not always work out as planned.

Wrinkled
was not one of
the things
I wanted to be
when I grew up.

And you won't always be right.

What was I thinking?

But at least you'll know it was your choice.

You're not the boss of me.